c.2

Death Adder

By Lincoln James

Gareth Stevens
Publishing

Please visit our Web site, www.garethstevens.com. For a free color catalog of all our high-quality books, call toll free 1-800-542-2595 or fax 1-877-542-2596.

Library of Congress Cataloging-in-Publication Data

James, Lincoln.
Death adder / Lincoln James.
    p. cm. — (Killer snakes)
Includes index.
ISBN 978-1-4339-4542-7 (pbk.)
ISBN 978-1-4339-4543-4 (6–pack)
ISBN 978-1-4339-4541-0 (library binding)
1. Acanthophis—Juvenile literature. I. Title.
QL666.O64J36 2011
597.96'4—dc22

                                        2010024992

First Edition

Published in 2011 by
Gareth Stevens Publishing
111 East 14th Street, Suite 349
New York, NY 10003

Designer: Michael J. Flynn
Editor: Greg Roza

Photo credits: Cover, pp. 1, (2–4, 6, 8, 10–12, 14, 16–18, 20–24 snake skin texture), 5, 9, 10–11, 21 Shutterstock.com; pp. 7, 16–17 Jason Edwards/National Geographic/Getty Images; pp. 13, 15 Ian Waldie/Getty Images; p. 19 Michael & Patricia Fogden/Minden Pictures/Getty Images.

Printed in the United States of America

CPSIA compliance information: Batch #CW11GS: For further information contact Gareth Stevens, New York, New York at 1-800-542-2595.

Contents

Boldface words appear in the glossary.

Meet the Death Adder

A death adder uses **venom** to kill animals. One bite from a death adder can even kill a person!

Death adders live in many different places. Some live near coasts. Some live where it is grassy. Some live in forests. Others live in deserts.

The southern death adder is the most common kind. It lives in eastern and southern Australia. It has brown **scales**. The desert death adder lives in central and western Australia. It has reddish-brown scales. Other kinds live in New Guinea and on nearby islands.

Australia

KEY
southern death adder
desert death adder

Other Adders

The word "adder" is often used to describe snakes in the viper family. Vipers have long **fangs** and powerful venom. Most have short, wide bodies. Death adders aren't vipers. They just look like them.

Size and Shape

Adult death adders have thick bodies. They are shorter than many other snakes. Most are between 1 and 2 feet (30 and 60 cm) long. At the end of a death adder's body is a short, thin tail. Its head is shaped like an arrow.

11

Baby Death Adders

A female death adder may have 10 to 30 live babies at one time! A newborn death adder is only a few inches (cm) long. Female death adders do not take care of their babies. Newborn death adders begin hunting for food right away.

13

Hidden Danger

Death adders hide in tall grass or in the sand. If an animal or person scares one, it will not **slither** away. It will **attack**! A death adder has two sharp fangs. The fangs shoot strong venom into an animal's body. Most animals die soon after.

15

Waiting for Food

Death adders hide and sleep during the day. They hunt at night. Death adders like to eat small animals such as mice, frogs, and birds. They do not search for food. They only attack animals that are nearby. Sometimes they wait days for a meal to pass by.

A death adder's tail looks like a worm. The snake lies with its tail near its head. Then it shakes its tail. When an animal tries to eat the tail, the death adder bites it. After the venom kills the animal, the death adder swallows it whole.

19

Death Adders and People

Some people think death adder venom might be used to make **medicines**. However, it is very hard to get venom from a death adder without getting bitten! A person can die from a death adder bite. They must take a drug right away to stop the venom.

Snake Facts
Death Adder

Length	1 to 2 feet (30 to 60 cm)
What It Eats	small animals such as mice, frogs, and birds
Where It Lives	Australia, New Guinea, and surrounding islands
Life Span	up to 9 years
Killer Fact	The cane toad, a **poisonous** animal, eats baby death adders. An adult death adder will die if it eats a cane toad!

Glossary

attack: to try to harm someone or something

fang: a long, sharp tooth

medicine: a drug taken to make a sick person well

poisonous: containing poison, which can hurt people or animals

scale: one of the flat plates that cover a snake's body

slither: to slide easily over the ground

venom: something a snake makes in its body that can harm other animals

For More Information

Books

Thomson, Sarah L. *Amazing Snakes!* New York, NY: HarperCollins Publishers, 2006.

White, Nancy. *Death Adders: Super Deadly!* New York, NY: Bearport Publishing, 2009.

Web Sites

Common Death Adder

australianmuseum.net.au/Common-Death-Adder
Read more about the southern death adder, which is also called the common death adder.

Wild Recon: Death Adder Venom

animal.discovery.com/videos/wild-recon-death-adder-venom.html
Watch an Animal Planet video about the death adder and its venom.

Index